... because we are all holding each other
through a dance of joy and love.

Phyllis Berenson

This is a book about hugging.

Hugging is an instinct, a natural response to feelings of affection, compassion, need, and joy.

Hugging is also a science, a simple method of support, healing, and growth, with measurable and remarkable results.

In its highest form, hugging is also an art.

Techniques of hugging are described here with a cheerful mix of whimsy and seriousness. May they serve as a framework for you to create your own experience and practice as a Hug Therapist.

THE
HUG THERAPY
BOOK

Kathleen Keating

Drawings by Mimi Noland

CompCare®
Publishers

2415 Annapolis Lane, Minneapolis, Minnesota 55441

Keating, Kathleen, 1938-
  The hug therapy book.

  1. Hugging. I. Title.
BF637.H83K4 1983   158'.2   82-22173
ISBN 0-89638-065-3

Cover and interior design by Kristen McDougall

Inquiries, orders, and catalog requests should be addressed to
CompCare Publishers
2415 Annapolis Lane
Minneapolis, Minnesota 55441
Call toll free 800/328-3330
(Minnesota residents 612/559-4800)

13   14
        90

I embrace with honor

> My daughter, Ann Maureen Keating,
> and all those at her special place of learning
> for the developmentally disabled,
> St. Vincent School in Santa Barbara, California
>
> and my son, Matthew Roy Keating

I embrace with gratitude

> Golda Clendenin, who inspired me
>
> My friends and colleagues at Woodview-Calabasas
> Hospital, who supported me
>
> Esalen Institute for teaching me
>
> David Gorton for believing in me

hug (hug) v.t. hugged, hugging, hugs.

1. to clasp or hold closely, especially in one's arms; embrace or enfold, as in affection
2. to cherish, hold fast
3. to keep very close to

hug n.

An affectionate embrace. (From Scandinavian, akin to old Norse *hugga*, to comfort, console.)

hug therapy

The practice of administering hugs for the purpose of curing or healing, or of preserving health. Treatment of dis-ease through the simple, physical means of hugging.

About hugging and huggers

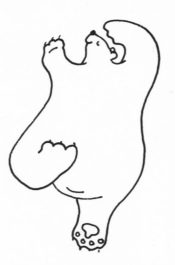

A hug makes you feel good all day.

Theory

Touch is not only nice. It's needed. Scientific research supports the theory that stimulation by touch is absolutely necessary for our physical as well as our emotional well-being.

Therapeutic touch, recognized as an essential tool for healing, is now part of nurses' training in several large medical centers. Touch is used to help relieve pain and depression and anxiety, to bolster patients' will to live, to help premature babies—who have been deprived of touch in their incubators—grow and thrive.

Various experiments have shown that touch can:

Make us feel better about ourselves and our surroundings;

Have a positive effect on children's language development and IQ;

Cause measurable physiological changes in the toucher and the touched.

We are just beginning to understand the power of touch.

While there are many forms of touching, we propose that hugging is a very special one that contributes in a major way to healing and health.

Rationale

HUGGING

Feels good

Dispels loneliness

Overcomes fears

Opens doors to feelings

Builds self-esteem ("Wow! *She* actually wants to hug *me!*")

Fosters altruism ("I can't believe it, but I actually *want* to hug that old son-of-a-gun!")

Slows down aging; huggers stay younger longer

Helps curb appetite; we eat less when we are nourished by hugs—and when our arms are busy wrapped around others

HUGGING ALSO

Eases tension

Fights insomnia

Keeps arm and shoulder muscles in condition

Provides stretching exercise if you are short

Provides stooping exercise if you are tall

Offers a wholesome alternative to promiscuity

Offers a healthy, safe alternative to alcohol and other drug abuse *(better hugs than drugs!)*

Affirms physical being

Is democratic; anyone is eligible for a hug

HUGGING ALSO

Is ecologically sound, does not upset the environment

Is energy-efficient, saves heat

Is portable

Requires no special equipment

Demands no special setting; anyplace from a doorstep to an executive conference room, from a church parlor to a football field, is a fine place for a hug!

Makes happy days happier

Makes impossible days possible

Imparts feelings of belonging

Fills up empty places in our lives

Keeps on working to dispense benefits even after the hug's release

Besides, hugging prevents war.

Qualifications

The qualifications for being a Hug Therapist and being a client are the same: just being.

Therapeutic hugging is a mutually healing process. In fact, hugger and hugged play interchangeable roles. As a Hug Therapist, you are open to the child within you who needs love, safety, support, caring, and play, and you are reaching out to the same needs in the other.

A Hug Therapist does not blame or judge. But he or she does recognize that many of us, in our standoffish society, have not learned to ask for the emotional support we need. If love or support—or play—has been skimpy since childhood, we may feel wounded. If the twistings of growing up have left us with low self-esteem, we may feel unlovable—unhuggable.

Hug Therapists can't solve all these problems, but they can respect the struggles and offer understanding, laughter, gentle words, and an abundance of hugs.

Hug Therapy is not just for the lonely or hurting ones. Hug Therapy can make the healthy healthier, the happy happier, and the most secure among us feel even more so.

Hugging is for everybody.

Anyone can be a Hug Therapist. But if you master the Types of Hugs and the Advanced Techniques presented in this book, you will develop further skills and confidence in your natural ability to share wonderful hugs.

Ethics and rules of conduct

When you are a truly professional Hug Therapist, you take full responsibility for what you say or do. Therefore the hugs you share must be thoughtful, respectful, and care-filled.

These are understood rules of conduct for Hug Therapists:

1. *Since Hug Therapy is always nonsexual, hug accordingly.* Be sure that the hugs you dispense are compassionate, not passionate. A caring, comforting, or playful hug is different from a lover's embrace. We usually recognize the difference.

No.

If you started out offering or wanting a supportive hug, and it has taken on overtones of greater physical intimacy, just recenter your feelings and thoughts on the original purpose of the hug—to give mutual support.

If you are clear about the kind of hug you are giving, the other hugger most likely will respond in kind. If not, you may want to have a talk about the importance of just-friendly hugs in your relationship.

Yes.

2. *Be certain you have permission before giving a hug.* Often permission to hug is implicit in a relationship. Your sweetheart or a close friend probably will welcome hugs almost any time. However you still need to respect the other's need for privacy and space.

Sometimes you will receive nonverbal permission from someone who wants a hug, and you respond spontaneously. Or pave the way to hugging with a simple comment like, "I would like to give you a hug." Respect the other's verbal and nonverbal messages. Most of the time you will be aware of what is needed and acceptable.

If you misread someone who did not find a hug comfortable, don't be concerned. For some, hugging is very hard; sometimes a sturdy trust must be built before they feel safe enough to hug. Although we Hug Therapists believe the gift of touch to be extremely important, the gift of acceptance is just as important!

Ask first.

3. *Also be sure to ask permission when <u>you</u> need a hug.* Hug Therapists are not only dispensers of hugs but recipients too. Huggers must sometimes be huggees. Hugging-for-health is a practice of sharing, rather than of just giving or just taking.

When you feel the need for a hug, say: "I would like a hug, if it's all right with you." Or, "I could really use a huge hug right now — would you oblige?" Or, "How about a hug before I go off to work (or to a meeting or a match or an interview or whatever). A post-hug "thank you" or "that felt good" is an important validation of the other's support.

May I have this hug?

4. Be responsible for expressing what you need and the way you want it. Blaming others because we're not getting what we need from them is a common mistake we make in our relationships. Some are naturally fine-tuned and intuitive about others' needs and comforts. But most of us—especially if we are busy worrying about our own insecurities—need direct, explicit communication.

If we want more hugs, fewer hugs, ten-second hugs, or two-minute-over-easy hugs—any kind of hug that may be different from what we're getting—we need to say so. Then we have to be willing to compromise as well as to realize that we won't always get exactly what we want when we want it.

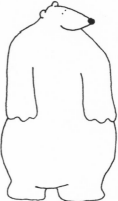

For some, hugging is very hard.

Contraindications

A MYTH AND A MODEL

While Hug Therapists are convinced that hugging is for everyone, a few doubters have trouble accepting Hug Therapy. They believe, erroneously, that the sole purpose of a hug is to build a relationship of physical intimacy.

A physically intimate embrace can be beautiful too, but it meets a different level of need. This kind of embrace will never replace a good old therapeutic hug! Even intimate partners need bundles of ordinary hugs too.

To keep little ones from acquiring this narrow view of hugs, hug them often—affectionately, supportively, playfully, and tenderly. Let them see parents and other adults hugging in these ways. Otherwise they may grow up believing that hugs are for lovers only, and that in order to be hugged—and huggable—one must be physically attracted to the other hugger.

A Hug Therapist makes every effort to share the broader understanding of touch and hugging and the faith that a day filled with hugs can bring untold satisfaction and serenity.

Fees

Hug Therapy is not free. The cost is the strength it requires to be vulnerable. The fee for hugging is the risk that our hugs will be rebuffed or misinterpreted.

When we are very young we are naturally open. We want to give love and touch as much as we want to get love and be touched. If we're deprived of love and touch, we become unwilling to pay the fee of vulnerability. Love held back can turn to pain.

Hug therapists can help ease this pain. When we risk our hugs, we affirm our wonderful ability to share. As we reach out and touch others, we are free to discover the compassion—along with the capacity for joy—that exists in all of us. As we become more spontaneous huggers and find such inner riches, the fees seem relatively small.

Thank goodness we have our softer sides.

Types of hugs

Bear hug

In the traditional bear hug (named for members of the family Ursidae, who do it best), one hugger usually is taller and broader than the other, but this is not necessary to sustain the emotional quality of bear-hugging. The taller hugger may stand straight or slightly curved over the shorter one, arms wrapped firmly around the other's shoulders. The shorter of the pair stands straight with head against the taller hugger's shoulder or chest, arms wrapped—also firmly!—around whatever area between waist and chest that they will reach. Bodies are touching in a powerful, strong squeeze that can last five to ten seconds or more.

We suggest you use skill and forbearance in making the hug firm rather than breathless. Always be considerate of your partner, no matter what style of hug you are sharing.

The feeling during a bear hug is warm, supportive, and secure.

Bear hugs are for:

Those who share a common feeling or a common cause.

Parents and offspring. Both need lots of reassuring bear hugs.

Grandparents and grandoffspring. Don't leave grandparents out of family bear hugs.

Friends (this includes marrieds and lovers, who hopefully are friends too).

Anyone who wants to say, wordlessly, "You're terrific!" Or, "I'm your friend; you can count on me." Or, "I share whatever pain or joy you're feeling."

What can a bear hug say for you?

The A-frame hug

Stand facing each other, wrapping arms around shoulders, sides of heads pressed together and bodies leaning forward and not touching at all below shoulder level. There. You have an A-frame hug. The length of time spent in the A formation is usually brief, since this is often a "hello" or "goodbye" hug.

The underlying feeling may be one of polite caring or detached warmth.

The A-frame hug is most appropriate for new acquaintances or professional colleagues, or in situations that require a degree of formality. Because it is relatively nonthreatening, it is comfortable for shy or unpracticed huggers.

This is a classic hug and should not be discounted because of its formal quality. It has broad application and is therefore beneficial to a wide range of huggers.

An A-frame hug is particularly apt for:

A great-aunt whom you haven't seen since you were a toddler.

Your spouse's employer's husband.

Your former academic adviser.

A new daughter-in-law.

Who else?

Like this.

Cheek hug

The cheek hug is a very tender, gentle hug that often has a spiritual quality. It can be experienced comfortably sitting down, standing up, or even with one sitting and one standing, as full body contact is not necessary.

If you are both seated, turn comfortably toward each other and press the sides of your faces together cheek to cheek. One hand may be on the other's back and the other supporting the back of the head to counteract the pressure of your cheek. Breathe slowly and deeply. Within a few seconds you will feel very relaxed. The cheek hug often stirs deep feelings of kindness, especially when participants are close friends.

A cheek hug is a tasteful way to:

Greet an elderly friend or relative who is seated.

Say a wordless "I'm sorry" about a friend's disappointment.

Share a friend's joy at a happy occasion, like a wedding or graduation. (This is a considerate hug for congratulating the principals in reception lines, since it does not tangle wedding veils or crush boutonnières.)

At what times would you proffer a cheek hug?

It often has a spiritual quality.

Sandwich hug

The sandwich hug is a lesser known variety, but once you experience its warmth and security, you'll want to share this one often.

This is a hug for three. Two face each other with the third in the middle facing either one of the others. Each of the two on the outside reaches toward the waist area of the other and hugs. The one in the center wraps arms around the waist of the facing hugger. As an option, the outside pair may hug around the shoulders and all three snuggle heads together. The bodies are touching cozily.

The sandwich hug gives the one in the middle an especially secure feeling, which is helpful if she or he is going through a difficult time and needs extra support.

The sandwich hug is handy for:

Three good friends.

A couple wishing to comfort someone.

Two parents and a child. The child may be very young, grown up, or any place between.

Make your own sandwich.

Grabber-squeezer hug

The grabber-squeezer hug holds the record for brevity. One hugger runs up to and throws arms about another, gives a fast squeeze before letting go, then dashes off. The one so hugged must be alert in giving a squeeze in return, in order to receive maximum benefit from this hug.

In a variation of the grabber-squeezer, choreographically more difficult, both run toward each other and give a quick, simultaneous squeeze. Safety note: Avoid a collision course. The full-force crash of two bodies who have hurtled together or the knocking of two heads may negate some of the good feelings!

Feelings vary with the situation, but often the grabber-squeezer is accompanied by a sense of affectionate

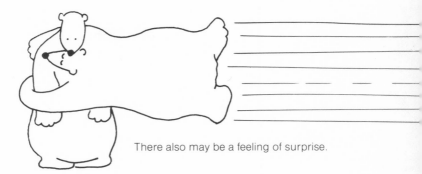

There also may be a feeling of surprise.

distraction because one or both of the huggers are rushed. If the huggee is not expecting it, there also may be a feeling of surprise.

Grab-and-squeeze hugging is a practical way to work in a lot of fast hugging when you're on a tight schedule. For more effective stress management, also include a liberal sprinkling of hugs that are gentler and last longer.

Use the grabber-squeezer:

> In the workshop or the kitchen.

> To wish someone luck before a performance.

> As a silent translation of the words "I like you a lot, but I'm in a terrible hurry!"

How can the grabber-squeezer fit into your life?

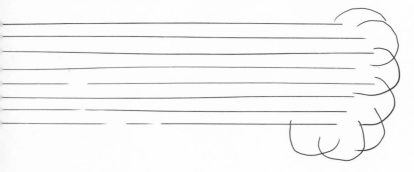

Group hug

The group hug is a very popular hug for good friends sharing in an activity or project. As Hug Therapists, we would like the group hug to be better known and more often applied, just because it feels so good.

The group forms a circle—its members standing as close together as possible, arms around shoulders or waists—and squeezes. In a variation, group hug participants, holding each other as above, move in toward the center, shrinking the circle. They huddle together for several moments, then back up and break apart with a cheer or sigh or a quick, parting squeeze.

Besides good feelings of support, security, and affection, group hugs often impart a sense of unity and universal belonging.

Group hugs are good for:

    Growth groups.

    Support groups.

    Classmates, teammates.

    Hardworking committees.

    Any bunch you like.

When would your group welcome a hug like this?

A group hug often imparts a sense of universal belonging.

Side-to-side hug

The side-to-side hug, or the lateral squeeze, is a great hug to get and give while walking along together. As you stroll side by side with an arm around the other's waist or over the shoulder, once in a while give a generous squeeze.

This is also a merry and playful hug for those moments when you are standing in line with a friend. It makes queuing up a pleasure!

The side-to-side hug provides a joyful moment while:

Walking to a bus.

On a hike or an archaeological dig.

Waiting to get into a Saturday night movie or to register for next term's classes.

When could you use a side-to-side hug?

Back-to-front hug

In the back-to-front hug (also known as the waist-grabber), the hugger approaches the other from the back, folds arms around his or her waist and gives a gentle hug.

The back-to-front waist-grabber is the perfect hug to give someone who is peeling potatoes, scrubbing pans over a kitchen sink, or otherwise engaged in some routine stand-up chore. A somewhat old-fashioned hug, this was practiced more extensively before the invention of the automatic dishwasher. But most of the time a waist-grabber is still welcome as a brief, playful gesture. The feeling behind it is happy and supportive.*

*Even more supportive would be the back-to-front hug *followed by* the picking up of a dishtowel and applying it to the pans.

Back-to-front hugs are for:

    Househusbands, housewives, and other live-ins.

    Co-workers on an assembly line.

    Friends whose occupations require that they face
    mostly in one direction—like raspberry-pickers
    or mail-sorters.

*Do you know someone who would appreciate a
waist-grabber?*

Heart-centered hug

Many consider the heart-centered hug to be the highest form of hugging, and official Hug Therapists feel, too, that it is indeed very powerful.

The heart-centered hug begins with direct eye contact as the two huggers stand facing each other. Then the arms are wrapped around shoulders or back. Heads are together, and there is full body contact. The hug is firm, yet gentle. As the two breathe slowly and easily together, they focus on the compassion that is flowing from one heart into the other.

There is no time limit on this hug; it may last several moments, shutting out all nearby distractions. The heart-centered hug is full and lingering, caring and tender, open and genuine, supportive and strong.

The heart-centered hug acknowledges that place at the center of each of us where—if we're open to it—pure, unconditional love may be found.

The heart-centered hug feels right:

> When the huggers are very old friends with a long history of crisscrossing paths.

> When the huggers are very new friends brought together by a shared experience and a strong, shared emotion.

When might you share a heart-centered hug?

It may last several moments, shutting out all distractions.

Custom-tailored hug

The most effective hug for you is the hug that feels right, considering the setting, the situation, the one you are with, and what you personally need from the hug (affection, strength and support, reaffirmation of a bond of friendship, relaxation, or any other good feeling that a hug can bring.)

Sometimes a custom-tailored hug is called for, as in the case of an extra-tall hugger and a very short huggee (or vice versa). Or when the hug, in order to please both parties equally, has to include a jealous pet or a favorite toy too.

Be creative. True Hug Therapists do not let circumstances stand in their way.

A custom-tailored hug may have to include a favorite toy.

Hugs: where, when, why

Environments

A place of beauty enhances the experience of hugging. Whatever setting you consider beautiful—a peaceful country path on a warm, clear day or a scrap of green park that opens a city to the sky—can make the hug you share with a friend even more special.

However, if the setting seems shabby or bleak, it can be totally transformed just because you are sharing a hug.

Anyplace is the right place for hugging when the heart is open.

A hug transforms a bleak setting . . .

. . . into a lovely place.

Time of day

Some are morning, up-and-at-'em huggers. Some are evening, thank-heaven-the-day-is-over huggers. Some like to hug at high noon on lunch hours or at teatime. Although routine hugs are fine, sometimes the most appreciated hugs happen spontaneously at unexpected moments.

The feelings that bring on a hug—affection, sympathy, caring, just plain joy—can happen at any time of day. So can hug situations, like bumping into an old school friend at an airport. True Hug Therapists will entertain the idea of a hug at any time. And hugs scattered through the day will help to maintain a sense of well-being, belonging, and self-esteem.

Friendship

Compassion

Joy

Feelings that bring on a hug . . .

... can happen any time.

Sound effects

A hug may be accompanied by a moment of stillness.
Or it may include expressions of pleasure, like these:

(Sigh)

Whoopee!

That's nice.

Thank you. I needed that.

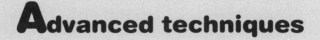

Advanced techniques

Visualization

Visualization is a powerful technique for learning and change. One way we learn is through repeated imprintings on our minds — not only of what we actually view in the world around us, but also of pictures we see in our imaginations. Imagined pictures, which can affect us as strongly as reality, sometimes even set off physical responses.

Think about slicing a juicy lemon and squeezing the tart juice into your mouth. Your mouth waters at the very thought. You may detect a sour taste, too. You have the sensation of sucking a lemon even though there's no real lemon anywhere in sight.

Now try visualizing yourself hugging somebody. Let this imagined hug register in your mind as a nourishing experience. A mind picture like this can teach you to see yourself as someone who is at ease giving and getting warm, caring hugs.

In guided imagery, you plan or guide the direction you'd like your imagination to take. So let's say you would like to be comfortable greeting a friend with a heart-centered hug. Sit in a comfortable, quiet place and close your eyes. Breathe slowly and deeply four or five times and let your body relax totally. Imagine yourself walking along and meeting a good friend. Picture the two of you saying hello by putting your arms around each other and sharing a heart-centered hug.

Keep the picture in your mind as you sense good feelings of affection and warmth. It is important to put the imagined picture and the feelings together.

Or use guided imagery when you are feeling the need for support after a stressful day. Visualize a favorite friend who is also a good hugger giving you a very fond and supportive hug. Imagine that friend holding you and offering you reassurance and love. Keep the picture and the feelings in your mind for as long as you need comfort.

An imagined hug is a nourishing experience.

Zen hugging

You can use any type of hug for Zen hugging. Our
favorites are the cheek-to-cheek hug or the heart-
centered hug. A very connected touch—a feet-to-feet
and hands-to-hands touch, for instance—will do
fine, too.

Your eyes may be open or closed. Focus on your
breathing, and allow it to become even and deep. You
will begin to feel yourself relaxing. You are centered
in the present moment. Let go of all thinking. All that
is present is the experience of your senses.

You are aware of the warmth you are sharing, of your breath moving in and out, of the touch of the other person, of the air on your skin. Relax. Be suspended in time. The longer you are able to relax in the present moment, the deeper will be your experience of the hug or the touching.

Peace.

You are centered in the present moment.

That extra touch

Hugging is just one kind of therapeutic touching. There are others too, as touch research has confirmed.

You may want to combine hugging with another nourishing kind of platonic touching, such as gentle stroking or patting.

There are other kinds of therapeutic touching too.

Institute of hug therapy

We believe more must be done to break down the cultural and emotional barriers that prevent us from experiencing the healthy nourishment of touching and hugging. The establishment of the Institute of Hug Therapy is our whimsical, but earnest, contribution to that effort.

Becoming a member of the Institute of Hug Therapy is easy. Just believe in the power of hugging! Wear the title of Hug Therapist proudly. Tell others about hugging for health. Spread the pro-hug philosophy wherever you go.

Hugging should not be something you do once in a while, at family reunions or birthdays or when one of your teammates makes a goal. Our hope is that hugging will become commonplace, without detracting from the specialness of each separate hug.

Institute of Hug Therapy
Certificate of Membership

This is to certify that

_____

name

has completed the course of study offered in *The Hug Therapy Book* and is now a practicing Hug Therapist dedicated to the furtherance of hugging for health on an international scale.

Hug often. Hug well.

About the author

Kathleen Keating, R.N., M.A., is a mental health counselor and consultant in private practice in California. She conducts seminars and workshops all over the country on health and well-being, stress management, parent education, communication and problem-solving skills, and group dynamics. Her experience also includes biofeedback research and consulting and administration in therapeutic communities. A former director of inservice education and of community relations for Woodview-Calabasas Hospital in Calabasas, California, she has participated in nearly fifty special seminars on a breadth of topics—from Gestalt therapy to psychosynthesis.

The theme of her life is, she says, "to feel, know, and teach the many dimensions of love: courage to struggle; vulnerability to give and to receive; sensitivity to compassion and the power of anger; openness to the delight of play and the deep, deep pleasure of a warm embrace."

For more copies of *The Hug Therapy Book, Hug Therapy 2,* or *Hug Therapy* calendars, ask your bookseller. Books and calendars, along with hug cards, are also available from CompCare Publishers, 2415 Annapolis Lane, Minneapolis, MN 55441. In Minnesota call 612/559-4800. Toll free outside Minnesota: 800/328-3330.

"I want a world where people are respected for the ease and warmth of their melting... rather than the strength of their walls."

> Clint Weyand
> from *My Miracle Is You*
> (Being Books)

"Since our beginnings we have been acquiring knowledge and wisdom. We have been Homo Sapiens—knowing human. Now we have enough new knowledge to enter our next dimension, as Homo Biologicus—biological human. What does our biological organism require to function at its optimum, its most joyful? We now have scientific evidence that among its powerful needs is touching—human contact. Often making contact with another, The New Human Being—a combination of Homo Sapiens and Homo Biologicus—will add to the world's health and joys as the pioneer of a more loving, nurturing society."

Helen Colton
author of *The Gift of Touch* (G. P. Putnam's Sons)

"Hugging fosters a feeling of self-worth; it makes you more accepting of yourself. . . . By helping you realize that you are a good person—a *huggable* person—it makes you want to take better care of that good person in order to keep that good person on the planet as long as possible."

Barbara Toohey & June Bierman
from *The Diabetic's Total Health Book*
(J. P. Tarcher)

Name: _____
Diagnosis: Touch deprivation
Treatment Plan: An abundance of hugs
Prognosis: Excellent